T0304998

HONJOK

This edition published in 2020 by
Eddison Books Limited
www.eddisonbooks.com

British Library Cataloguing-in-Publication data available on request.

ISBN 978-1-85906-459-7

10 9 8 7 6 5 4 3 2 1

Printed in Europe

HONJŎK

The art of living alone

Francie Healey
Introduction by Crystal Tai

Eddison Books Ltd

CONTENTS

1

TRiBES OF ONE

WHO ARE SOUTH KOREA'S HONJOK?

In 2017 the term 'honjok' (pronounced hon-juk) emerged as a counter-culture buzzword in South Korea, when droves of young Koreans began using it as a hashtag to describe themselves and their activities. 'Hon' is short for 'honja', meaning alone; 'jok' means tribe. Simply put, 'honjok' means 'tribe of one'.

While there is no one exact sociological definition for the term or the group it describes, the honjok generally opt to do activities alone and make the most of their independence, rejecting South Korea's collectivistic social values which place a higher value on the needs and desires of the community over the individual. This includes pushing back against the pressure of forming a traditional atomic family unit – often foregoing marriage and choosing to live alone on their own terms.

In a country where most of the older generation married young and expect millennials to follow suit in order to continue family lines, this is especially controversial. The nation's birth rate is already among the lowest in the world with only 95 children born per every 100 women, and by some estimates South Koreans are even facing 'natural extinction' by 2750.

And yet while the honjok have made the conscious decision to live alone, eat alone ('honjok, honbap' means 'tribe of one, meal for one') and spend time enjoying activities on their own, it's also clear that some of this was borne out of circumstance.

The honjok movement arose during a time of frustration for many young Koreans. After years of competing within a sluggish economy, as well as a lack of job opportunity and social mobility, the nation's youth despaired of what might become of them. Many felt they had no choice but to choose the honjok life. The number of single-person households in Seoul makes up almost one third of all households in the city at 31.6 per cent, according to data from April 2019, and is only slated to rise. By 2026, single-person households will rise to 36.3 per cent of total households – making up the greatest majority in the nation, according to Statistics Korea.

And Korea is not alone. In the US, for instance, single-person households are more commonplace than ever –comprising 28 per cent of households in 2018. In other Western countries like the UK and Sweden, more and more people spend time on their own and live alone. In Sweden, 1.8 million people, or 39.2 per cent of all households, and 17.8 per cent of the population was comprised of single-person households in 2017.

MODERN KOREA

These days, it's all too easy to see only the phenomenal and successful rise of Korea's K-wave, comprising K-pop, K-dramas, K-fashion, K-beauty – all of which denote Korea's current status as a cultural superpower, and the shiny, glossed-over newness of it all. It's easy to look past the torrid and still quite raw history that has influenced many aspects of Korea today and gave rise to the complex issues undercutting society.

For hundreds of years, South Korea and North Korea existed as a unified sovereign empire under the Joseon dynasty (1392–1920), during which it was a nominal tributary to China. From the fifteenth to sixteenth centuries, the kingdom flourished with the development of its own technologies, arts, and culture. Neo-Confucianism was the predominant ideology, and strict social classes existed, ranging from the *yangban*, or nobles, to the *nobi*, or indentured servants and slaves.

By the nineteenth century, however, Korea was nicknamed the 'hermit kingdom', due to its reluctance to open up after it faced a series of invasions by Japan. The country became annexed by its neighbour and remained under Japanese occupation from 1910 to 1945. During this time, over five million Koreans became conscripted into forced labour under the Japanese. According to some records, 400,000 of them died. Meanwhile, hundreds of thousands of women

from Korea and neighbouring China were forced into sexual slavery, operating as 'comfort women' for the Japanese military – an issue that remains contentious and a source of conflict between Japan and Korea today.

Korean culture was suppressed as Japanese became the main language used in many areas of life, including academia, and industries were exploited as Korean resources were produced for and given to Japan. This period of cultural oppression ended with the surrender of Japan at the end of World War II in 1945. Korea was split into two administrations along the 38th parallel: The North, which was overseen by the Soviet Union, and the South, which became governed by the US.

During the Korean War, from 1950 to 1953, the two sides fought to gain control of the other. Each was backed by its governing Western superpower, and over 1.2 million died in a process that eventually ended in a stalemate, with both sides divided by the same boundary as before.

To this day, the Koreans remain divided, with husbands and wives, parents and children, siblings and other family groups still separated from one another. Although progress has been made over the years and the two sides have met, an ever-present North Korean threat of nuclear war continues to loom over the peninsula.

Despite its tragic modern history, South Korea experienced rapid economic development in the years following the Korean War. Between 1980 and 1990, the nation had the fastest-growing GDP in the world. During this time, however, the country came under the rule of authoritarian dictatorship regimes, such as that of former president Park Chung-hee (1963–1979) and military autocrat Chun Doo-hwan (1980–1988), which were marred by civilian uprisings, bloody clashes, and crackdowns, leading to the deaths of hundreds of protestors, such as during the 1980 Gwangju Uprising. In recent years, too, South Korea has been gripped by a series of tumultuous social and political protests.

The fall of former president Park Geun-hye in late 2016 shocked the nation. Daughter of the late dictator Park Chung-hee, she became embroiled in a scandal over her involvement in a bizarre corruption, exposing her close ties with a purported cult, and her role in bribing Korea's powerful *chaebol* (family-owned conglomerates), among other abuses of power.

In that same year, a young woman was murdered in Gangnam, Seoul's commercial district, by a stranger who confessed to committing the act out of a hatred for women. These events, together with the frustrations of young people struggling to survive within South Korea's ultra-competitive environment, became important catalysts for such trends as the honjok movement, formed out of mounting dissatisfaction and existential concerns.

FRUSTRATING SOCIAL HIERARCHIES

South Korea is often cited as a neo-Confucian culture similar to that of China, Japan, and much of East Asia. Neo-Confucianism was created out of attempts to merge the rational aspects of Confucianism with the less religious or mystical philosophies of Taoism and Buddhism, to form one coherent new school of thought. While its name sounds new, if not innovative, neo-Confucianism actually dates back to the Chinese Tang dynasty of 618–907 AD.

In Korea, neo-Confucianism was adopted as the state ideology of the Joseon dynasty, which lasted from 1392 to 1910. According to the ideology, elders were often expected to be treated with reverence, children were expected to be filial, and women were relegated to roles that were little more than being good mothers and good wives.

Today, in many aspects of society, South Koreans adhere to a rigid social hierarchy both in language and in daily interactions. Those who grew up in the '80s and '90s were often subjected to what Westerners might consider arbitrary, even shocking, sets of standards. In elementary schools, for example, students would be lined up and numbered according to their height – with the tallest and shortest at each end. As well as height still being an obsession, a great deal of importance is also placed on appearance, and the perceived attractiveness of young Koreans contributes to their social mobility. Until recently, most job applicants still included a photo with their resumés. While skills are assessed, a candidate's looks also impact their chances of being hired.

For generations, young South Koreans were told to pursue the 'Korean dream', a set of goals not unlike the American Dream taken up in the US during the McCarthy era of the 1950s. Study hard, graduate, get a job, get married, buy a house, have children... Many, if not most, followed this path, donning uniform-style black suits, dispersing into the 'real world' but finding such goals largely impossible to achieve. And for the lucky minority who did succeed, many discovered the reality of the success was not as it seemed.

Honjok invites us to
consider who we are outside
our established social and
cultural norms.

Today, most young South Koreans spend their teens and twenties studying and pursuing higher education, a set of certificates and licences in order to qualify for low-paying, entry-level office jobs at local conglomerates such as LG, Hyundai, and Samsung. Such work, while tedious and demanding, is framed as the only path for success. And despite the low salaries, such jobs are not easily available either.

THE RISE OF KOREAN FEMINISM

The emergence of South Korean feminism – and, linked to that, the rise of individualism – is another important factor that has influenced honjok culture, in particular South Korea's #NoMarriage movement. A growing number of women are choosing to stay single to maintain their own sense of independence and autonomy in the context of sexist and outdated societal views that women are best suited to becoming mothers and homemakers.

In a May 2018 *Vice* article, 'The death of romance and the rise of the "loner" in collectivist South Korea', Michael Hurt, a sociologist and research professor at the University of Seoul, said women have been forced to choose between careers or marriage. 'The traditional way of dealing with women in the workplace is you have a baby, and you're fired,' Hurt said in the article.

Traditionally, married women are expected to be dutiful and doting daughters-in-law, who do all

the cooking, cleaning, serving, and make all the preparations at family events. University student Kim Seo-Yeon says she has even heard of wives boycotting family holidays like *Chuseok* (Korean Thanksgiving) because of the extreme workload they are expected to take on, in addition to their usual household chores and emotional labour. 'I read an article by a woman who refused to participate in these events. She didn't want to be treated like a slave so she avoided these events for ten years,' she said, adding that the family eventually realized this was not a question of laziness but equality, and now no longer expect such contributions. 'South Korea experienced rapid economic growth which was unprecedented... The economy and material wealth developed so fast but psychologically and culturally, people are the same,' said Kim. 'This is reflected in the expectations that come with marriage.'

Data from Korea's national statistics agency reported that in 2010, 64.7 per cent of women in South Korea believed marriage was a necessity for women. In 2018, only 48.1 per cent agreed with this response.

Baeck Ha-na, together with co-host Jung Se-young, operates a YouTube channel in English called 'Solo-darity', promotes living alone and rejects the notion that she must marry and produce children to be considered successful. In a Bloomberg News July 2019 article, 'The #NoMarriage movement is adding to Korea's economic woes', she said: 'Society made me feel like a failure for being in my 30s and not yet a wife or a mother. Instead of belonging to someone, I now have a more ambitious future for myself'.

Spurred by Baeck's and Jung's activism, people are increasingly using the hashtag #NoMarriage to claim their autonomy and speak out against the push for women to have children, a rising concern for South Korea's government as the birth rate continues to drop.

South Korea's birth rate dropped in 2018 to .98 – less than one baby per woman, according to the most recent government report. The rate is among the lowest in the world and the lowest since the government began tracking rates in 1970.

According to a 2019 survey by matchmaking agency Duo Info Corp, 23.1 per cent of single respondents said they did not want to have children after marriage. Among them, a greater number of women, compared with men, said they had no plans for children. While heteronormative marriages are legal, gay marriage and other non-binary marital and romantic arrangements are still largely taboo in this conservative country. Also according to Duo, South Korean women married on average at 33.4 years old, and men at 36 years old. More than 90 per cent of men were older than their wives.

For those like 26-year-old Jenna Park, dating is hard enough, let alone the expectations within most marriages. 'Women are realizing what their rights are, and how they've been treated by men. But men are used to the ways things were in the past,' she says.

South Korea's burgeoning #MeToo movement is credited with the rise of local feminism. The movement first erupted in early 2018, after Seo Ji-hyun, a female prosecutor, went public with her allegations of sexual harassment against her former employer.

Around the same time, the nation began grappling with a spycam epidemic. Illicit hidden-camera crimes, from revenge porn uploaded onto free-streaming sites by former partners, to hidden cameras in public toilets and hotel rooms, to prominent K-pop stars filming intimate encounters without the woman's consent, were exposed. South Korean women began protesting both online and offline against their victimization and subsequent shaming, as well as the perceived lack of seriousness with which they felt these issues were being tackled by the authorities. Law enforcement has also been called to account.

ESCAPE THE CORSET

Many began to question the level of lookism (discrimination based on a person's appearance), which was so pervasive in South Korean society. As in much of the world, youth, beauty, and style impact how women are viewed, and beauty remains a crucial aspect of one's social capital in South Korea. It has one of the highest plastic surgery rates in the world, and, according to a poll by Gallup Korea, one in three women between the ages of 19 to 29 admit to having gone under the knife. So it was unexpected when South Korean women launched the anti-lookism movement Escape the Corset. It began largely online, with bloggers and Instagrammers declaring they would no longer adhere to rigid and monolithic beauty standards of white skin, double eyelids, small sharp noses, and V-line faces. Some women even documented themselves destroying their makeup and rejected long feminine hairstyles and clothing, which they felt objectified them through the male gaze.

'Women are deemed unworthy if they don't meet certain beauty standards,' said a Korean feminism scholar studying at Harvard University, who agreed to speak on the condition of anonymity. 'Men have it so much easier when it comes to choosing their partners,' she said, adding that K-pop girl groups often embody this caricature of a 'perfect female partner'. 'They need to be skinny, fair, and doll-faced, and their personality is always very happy, supportive – a perverse version of an imaginary wife or girlfriend men want to have.'

But beauty and marriage are not goals for many South Korean women today. Career and independence take precedence, and not being able to continue one's career is seen as the biggest obstacle to marriage.

From the disillusionment amid recent political upheaval, to the tremendous amount of competition faced in school and while job-hunting, as well as the lack of social mobility and opportunity, especially for women, and the growing realization of the myriad gendered expectations they must adhere to – this is how South Korea's honjok came to be.

GLOBAL TRIBES OF ONE

While some of the issues behind the honjok movement are unique to South Korea, it is evident that the movement does not exist in isolation. Under different terms, it is now a growing phenomenon in many societies around the world. All over the world, due to a unique set of factors including the global economic recession, the rise of individualism and feminism, social media and technology, and the #MeToo movement, it's fair to say a global movement of tribes of one has emerged.

Eric Klinenberg, a professor of sociology and director of the Institute of Public Knowledge at New

York University, researched the global trend of people living solo across the world in his 2012 book, *Going Solo, The Extraordinary Rise and Surprising Appeal of Living Alone.*

Klinenberg cited social changes – 'the emergence of the individual, the rising status of women, the growth of cities, the development of communications technologies and the expansion of the life course' – as driving forces for the move towards living alone. 'At this point in history it's clear that living alone will be an enduring feature of the contemporary developed world,' he wrote.

He also spent time looking into the social structures of Sweden, which has the highest rate of people living alone at 39.2 per cent of households in 2017 and also provides needed resources to support individual living, including residential buildings that promote communal living among singles.

Even in places where the government are less likely to subsidize younger singles, solo households are becoming more commonplace. In Asia, where singles have been disparaged – called 'leftover women' and 'bare branches' men in China, and 'Christmas cake' (like an old pastry) in Japan – more people are striking out on their own these days.

Just like in South Korea, women in China are choosing to marry later in life, or not at all. Some women in Japan participate in a new trend of solo

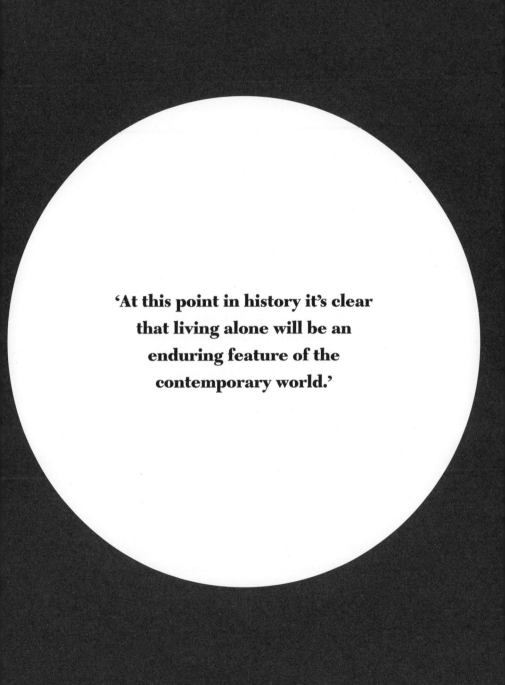

'At this point in history it's clear that living alone will be an enduring feature of the contemporary world.'

weddings as a way to recognize and honour their choice to live a single life.

Beyond marital status, compared with other parts of the world, the idea of spending time alone is very acceptable in Japan. Though not as well-known as honjok, the term 'ohitorisama' (on your own) evolved out of the growing popularity of one-person activities, such as eating and reading alone, and, more radically, going on trips alone and out for solo karaoke.

While not as dynamic as Korea's proud self-proclaimed honjok, Japan is leading the solo activity movement with entire industries including restaurants and entertainment facilities developing out of the demand for one-person activities.

What's truly innovative about Japan's ohitorisama culture is that it's not just for single people or those who live alone. Lots of people in relationships and those who live with families also engage in it too. It's become a way to recharge on your own.

VIEWS OF LONELINESS AND THE SELF

While the concept of individualism has been around since the 1800s, views on individualism and solitude and loneliness were truly propelled forward by thinkers like Hannah Arendt, a German-Jewish philosopher who wrote on political theory, and often on the individual and on society between the 1920s until her death in 1975.

Arendt believed that solitude was not so much a lonely activity as it was one in which you keep yourself company. And so, 'loneliness comes about when I am one and without company or when you don't offer yourself what you need in terms of companionship,' she wrote.

She believed that despite all our endless distractions and attempts to keep ourselves from socializing with ourselves, we would ultimately need to confront who we were. The self is the only one from whom you can never get away, she once wrote, unless you cease to exist.

Related to this notion of confronting yourself, the school of existentialism, a philosophy that championed a person's uniqueness and ability to think as an individual, and which held authenticity as our greatest virtue, also advocated that loneliness is simply an essential part of being human.

Early twentieth century philosophers such as Soren Kierkegaard, Jean-Paul Sartre and Friedrich Nietzsche all believed that we exist as separate beings, arriving in the world alone, journeying through life alone and departing alone. 'If you are lonely when you are alone, you are in bad company,' Sartre is often famously quoted for having said.

And yet loneliness was the essence of human existence, according to Sartre and his peers. Because in realizing that we are on our own, we realize we are in control of ourselves, and therefore responsible for what we do and ultimately for creating our own purpose in life.

While loneliness brings suffering and sadness, it is also inevitable, and a condition we must learn to accept and derive meaning from if we are to lead a meaningful existence. In this regard, existentialists believed that we should embrace our aloneness in this world, and find answers to questions such as life's true meaning, and how one uses freedom to define this and themselves. 'Existence precedes essence,' Sartre famously quipped, meaning that we exist, and therefore we must find our own purpose and direction. All responsibility for seeking this meaning in life comes upon ourselves.

The loneliness of this choice can be frightening and overwhelming, but it can also be immensely empowering. Loneliness becomes a decision. Do we take this uncomfortable feeling and find a way to distract ourselves and forget about it by engaging with paths of life without truly examining each choice we make, or do we navigate further down this and see what creativity and freedom it brings us closer towards?

Famously solitary writers like Ralph Waldo Emerson and Henry David Thoreau wrote about the importance of individualism in their art. 'Insist on one's self; never imitate,' wrote Emerson. 'Your own gift you can present every moment with the cumulative force of a whole life's cultivation; but of the adopted talent of another you have only an extemporaneous half possession. That which each can do best, none but his Maker can teach him.'

In *Walden*, or *Life in the Woods*, by Thoreau, the essayist writes about the contentment he has found while living alone in the countryside.

'Men frequently say to me, "I should think you would feel lonesome down there, and want to be nearer to folks, rainy and snowy days and nights especially",' he wrote. 'I am tempted to reply to such – "This whole earth which we inhabit is but a point in space. How far apart, think you, dwell the two most distant inhabitants of yonder star, the breadth of whose disk cannot be appreciated by our instruments? Why should I feel lonely?"'

It was in nature, while enjoying 'the friendship of the seasons' that Thoreau felt most connected with the world. 'I have never felt lonesome, or in the least oppressed by a sense of solitude, but once, and that was a few weeks after I came to the woods, when, for an hour, I doubted if the near neighborhood of man was not essential to a serene and healthy life. To be alone was something unpleasant,' he wrote.

With the absence of humans and civilization around him, Thoreau came to realize that the presence of the natural world kept him company. Little by little, he began to notice and appreciate the sights, sounds and sensations he'd scarcely noticed before. 'In the midst of a gentle rain while these thoughts prevailed, I was suddenly sensible of such sweet and beneficent society in Nature, in the very pattering of the drops, and in every sound and sight around my house, an infinite and uncountable friendliness all at once like an atmosphere sustaining me, as made the fancied advantages of human neighbourhood insignificant, and I have never thought of them since,' he wrote.

Sooyoun Kim grew up the youngest of five children in a social family in Seoul. In her young adulthood, she surrounded herself with people, constantly dating or socializing with friends. She was never alone. When she began meditating, she realized she hadn't tuned into herself before and felt more alone in the company of others. 'The great discovery of being alone and finding myself for the first time was a sort of enlightenment,' says the 47-year-old who lives by herself in Tongyong now.

Kim has found a new connection with nature as a result of her solitary life. She says she doesn't feel the need to engage in superficial conversations with people when she can talk to the trees or birds. Her solitude has actually enhanced her relationships with others because she's able to be more authentic and less superficial. She feels less lonely – even when she's alone – being true to herself.

SOCIAL GROUPS

Throughout life, many of us form bonds with groups of people with whom we feel a sense of belonging. According to Michael Hurt, social tribes are people who become united around a common interest or affiliation.

For many of us, it's in our early teens that we begin to strike out on our own, looking for like-minded people who share the same interests in cultural and recreational hobbies, such as the same genre of music, sports, types of games or puzzles. From the so-called band geeks, to the popular people, to the stoners out in the parking lot, this is how the quintessential cliques of high school are formed.

In these social tribes, we try to present ourselves in a certain way in order to fit in better and attain a better sense of belonging. We also compare ourselves to other members of the group to ensure that we fit the identity or image of the group.

As adults, we continue to seek our tribes, though this may become diversified and manifest itself in different ways. With the rise of leisure time, and thanks to technology taking over what were largely time-consuming chores and errands, such as washing clothes and the like, and despite the high level of productivity at work in many societies, we have much more leisure time than before – and with that, more time to explore and form social tribes.

With the advent of social media and other technologies, we have never been exposed to so many different platforms and sites through which we can meet others with similar tastes and interests.

What's fascinating is that this has led to the creation of the 'extended self'. The extended self was first formulated as a term in 1988 and is strongly linked with the concept of digital consumption, or how we use the Internet and related platforms. The extended self is the outside part of you that identifies with certain groups and tribes – for instance, you see yourself as a musician, and your extended self is part of a band that you play with every week.

The Internet has enabled us to create many versions of these extended selves, from the version of you that is shown on dating apps, to the version of you on discussion forums, to the version of you that chats with childhood friends who live faraway. In a sense, being able to be many versions of ourselves with many different people is wonderful and freeing, but it can also factor into role-playing and sometimes inauthenticity.

Michael Hurt calls these online expressions of self 'avatars'. He says that people can now hide behind their online icons/selves and engage in embarrassing behaviours that would otherwise be unacceptable. They can even find others who share the same non-politically correct views as themselves. Hence the emergence of mass-trolling cultures such as online flaming and doxxing. Through this more covert version of their extended selves, trolls can afford to be socially unacceptable and deviate from the need to seek belonging because no one knows who they really are, but at the same time they also find a community where they belong.

In her book *The Gifts of Imperfection*, vulnerability researcher Brene Brown defines belonging as an innate human desire to be part of something larger than us. 'Because this yearning is so primal, we often try to acquire it by fitting in and by seeking approval, which are not only hollow substitutes for belonging,

but often barriers to it,' she writes. Social tribes, whether for good or bad, help us find ways to express ourselves and identify with others.

And yet, true belonging can only happen when we present our authentic, imperfect selves to the world. According to Brown, 'Our sense of belonging can never be greater than our level of self-acceptance.'

Cultivating self-acceptance is a value some have found in the honjok life, regardless of whether others view honjoks negatively. However, Jang, who operates the website honjok.me, is working towards more validation of honjoks, creating the website to shift negative images of honjoks as losers or social outcasts and outsiders. 'I wanted to change these prejudiced notions to happiness, confidence, efficiency, reasonable lifestyle, and freedom,' Jang says.

Jang defines honjok as someone who stays faithful to oneself rather than spending time with other people. 'Before this word generally implied a socially awkward person. However, recently there is a positive change as voluntary "honjok", who confidently choose to remain alone and stay happy.'

BELONGING TO ONESELF

Michel de Montaigne, a significant philosopher of the French Renaissance stated, in *The Complete Essays*, 'The greatest thing in the world is to know how to belong to oneself.'

Honjok invites us to consider this sentiment, and who we are outside our established social and cultural norms. In this book we will reflect on the beauty of aloneness and the deep fulfilment that comes from investing in our inner life. This book will take you on a journey of self-reflection that will guide you inward through gentle inquiry and observation. You will learn about your true self, desires and needs while exploring the themes of solitude, self-worth and freedom from the inside out. Through this exploration the hope is that you will discover the gifts of belonging to yourself and feel more of a sense of peace by experiencing the fullness of who you really are.

'Belonging so fully to yourself that you're willing to stand alone is a wilderness – an untamed, unpredictable place of solitude and searching. It is a place as dangerous as it is breathtaking, a place as sought after as it is feared. The wilderness can often feel unholy because we can't control it, or what people think about our choice of whether to venture into that vastness or not. But it turns out to be the place of true belonging, and it's the bravest and most sacred place you will ever stand.'
– BRENE BROWN

2

A STATE OF MIND: LONELY OR ALONE?

LONELY OR ALONE?

How you view aloneness is a matter of personal perception. Some equate the word 'alone' with 'loneliness' and note an overlap between the two, others find serenity in the prospect of having space and time by themselves to truly be themselves, seeing being alone as a joyful experience with more freedom and less restriction.

The dictionary gives different definitions for the word 'alone'. At its most basic it is 'having no one else present; being without company'. Or it can mean being 'on your own' with a certain viewpoint or challenge, so you are 'unassisted' and 'without help'. The third definition of 'alone' is 'isolated and lonely'. That's quite a jump from a neutral meaning to a decidedly negative one.

Similarly, in our heads, we can define being alone as a positive, neutral or negative experience, depending on who we are, how we feel (about ourselves and others), our age and our personal life experience, cultural expectations and circumstances.

For instance, we might find ourselves growing more appreciative of alone time as we age. Certainly, there are all kinds of social and emotional interpretations of aloneness.

Conversely, the word 'lonely' is less subjective, although the experience of feeling lonely can be. In the dictionary, the definition of loneliness is specifically negative: 'Unhappy, because one has no friends or company'. Clearly, one of these words is dependent on perception; the other is simply sad, painful and absolute. Nobody wants to be lonely, yet plenty of people are content with being alone.

Certainly, if we consider the people we love most it's unlikely that anyone would want to think of them as lonely. Yet thinking of them being alone (with nobody else in their presence) is less daunting and more acceptable.

A STATE OF MIND

Whether we feel comfortable or uncomfortable with solitude, being alone is a state of mind. Some people love being alone in their own company, they cherish that time and space to themselves. Others struggle with being by themselves; they need to feel the comfort of company.

For some being alone is an opportunity to pause and reflect; a relief from the overwhelming pressures of daily life. For others, being alone equates to being unworthy of company and the associated quietness is something to fear rather than favour.

And therein lies the key: aloneness, or being alone, is a choice; loneliness is not.

LOOKING AT LONELINESS

Each of us - whether in a relationship or single - will likely experience feeling lonely at some point in our lives. It's a universal phenomenon. But what exactly is it? Loneliness, in general, comes from a lack of social support. It's an uncomfortable and unpleasant emotional response to isolation and how much social contact someone desires in relation to how much social contact they actually receive. Loneliness is the opposite of feeling content when you are by yourself. It's a kind of social pain; an unmet need; an anxious feeling about a lack of connection.

Loneliness is an empty hole, which can only be filled with connection, be that connection with others or connection with yourself. Whereas alone time can be quite the opposite, creating much-craved space, amid a world that's 'all go'. So, while there can be solace in solitude, loneliness is generally a more painful experience.

Ironically, technological advances have made us more able to have various needs met with minimal, if any, human interaction required. Paradoxically, we have the capacity to connect with much larger social

'Loneliness is the
poverty of self;
solitude is the
richness of self.'
— MAY SARTON

networks. In this way, heightened digital connection can actually cause us to experience less human connection, causing more loneliness despite the rise in virtual connection.

Loneliness is also caused by a situation or circumstance and, as such can be transient. Things like bereavement, break-ups, retirement, moving house or changing jobs can cause situational loneliness, as can circumstances such as being estranged from family, being a single parent with minimal adult contact, or being restricted from meeting people through disability or ill-health. Say you've moved to a new town and have been left alone while your partner goes to work, you might feel a sense of situational loneliness, but that feeling will pass.

However, if loneliness becomes chronic – defined by psychologists as lasting for more than two years – it can become both a mental and physical health risk.

AN UNHEALTHY FEELING
While time alone can bring positive health benefits, research has found loneliness can have an adverse effect on our health, with some reports suggesting loneliness can be as bad for our health as smoking or obesity. Consequently, in 2018, British Prime Minister Theresa May launched the first national campaign to end loneliness, calling it 'one of our greatest public

health challenges of our time.' According to research by the UK Office for National Statistics, younger adults aged 16–24 years reported feeling lonely more frequently than those in older age groups. And those with poorer health reported experiencing loneliness more often than those in good health.

Loneliness can lead to anxiety and depression, yet depression makes the sufferer less inclined to engage socially, which further feeds the lack of social interaction and increases the sense of loneliness, creating a perpetual loop of despair. And, because people feeling lonely or depressed can feel shame as a result of feeling this way, they can avoid actively seeking the help available.

Yet those who feel alone in this way are, ironically, not alone. There are others out there feeling lonely too. Indeed, according to statistics, between 5–10 per cent of the population have felt lonely during the past year, with younger people reporting more lonely and isolated days than middle-aged adults, despite having larger networks (Aging and Mental Health Survey, February 2019).

LACK OF CONNECTION

But you need not be alone to feel lonely. Loneliness is about the absence of connection, rather than the absence of people. For you can feel desperately lonely surrounded by people, yet quietly content when alone.

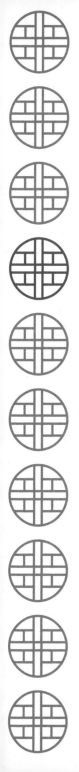

You can feel lonely despite being in a relationship. You can feel lonely despite being among friends. When you're lonely, you long for companionship and feel isolated, regardless of whether there are others around you. That's why people experiencing loneliness have often reported being surrounded by people yet never having felt lonelier.

Conversely, you can be completely alone, yet still feel connected to and supported by others. When you know you have supportive relationships, you can feel better about the prospect of being on your own. Equally, if you are someone who doesn't have a large support network, you could still be self-sufficient and happy enough in your own skin and in your own company that being alone does not cause you to feel lonely at all. That is how the honjok 'tribes of one' feel. However, if you do feel lonely, what can you do about it?

COMBATING LONELINESS

To soothe the social pain of loneliness you need to seek and develop social connections, while also learning to better connect with yourself. And you don't need to be in contact with hoards of people in order to feel less lonely.

According to research, we only need one or two people in our lives who allow us to be ourselves in order to feel sufficiently supported and connected.

44

DEALING WITH LONELINESS

The acknowledgement of lonely feelings is the first step to lift someone out of loneliness. Once you've accepted you are feeling lonely, you can take small steps towards making gentle changes, such as:

❊ Gaining confidence by learning how to better interact with people.

❊ Connecting online with like-minded people.

❊ Increasing social interaction by joining local classes or groups.

❊ Volunteering provides a wonderful way to meet new people, while helping others improves mental health and boosts wellbeing.

❊ Getting a pet or investigating pet therapy or 'animal assisted therapy'.

❊ Learning to like your own company by using self-compassion and self-acceptance interventions.

THE LONER LABEL

Honjok is an amalgamation of the words 'hon' (alone) and 'jok' (tribe) so is often referred to as a 'loner' tribe – a term which may seem contradictory given that a tribe consists of many people, rather than just one.

Indeed, a tribe connotes a community or family linked in some way, and, while this may seem at odds with the 'loner' label, honjoks are linked by a commonality in their desire to take time for themselves and live a life where solitude is sought-after and celebrated rather than fought against and rejected. This commonality makes them a tribe. So, while honjoks may choose to live alone, they share that desire with many other like-minded people.

And, with honjoks now becoming a significantly larger part of society, this tribe is growing, to the extent that there are now more single-person households in South Korea than households containing families. Consequently, the negative connotations of the 'loner' label are at odds with the more positive essence of what it is to be honjok.

LONER	HONJOK
Rejected by society/outcast	Rejects societal pressures and expectations to wed and start a family
Denounces and avoids human contact	Celebrates the individual over the group
Suffers loneliness	Enjoys taking time for themselves
Lack of fulfilment as hiding rather than thriving	Focus on self-fulfilment as a way to thrive over external validation and approval
Recluse and introvert	As likely to be an extrovert as an introvert but enjoys their own company
Lacks empathy as a result of being cut off	Improves empathy as a result of solo contemplation

The notion of a 'loner' has long been a negative and forlorn one. Given the tribal world we live in where community and belonging are seen as vital and innate human needs, the perception of a loner is in contrast to what society deems conducive to thriving. The loner label paints a picture of an anti-social person with no friends and no social life – a lonely hermit, be it through choice or circumstance. Loners are viewed as outcasts, either rejected by society or choosing to avoid human contact altogether; living on the edge of society. To be a loner is often judged as 'weird' or 'deviant' in some way, given that humans have always been social creatures.

Yet this label is in contrast to the positive loner lifestyle chosen by the rising number of honjoks, which, far from reducing their ability to thrive and feel fulfilled, enables it. The loner lifestyle has also been proven to be conducive to enhancing the creative and innovative powers of the human mind.

SUCCESSFUL LONERS

Despite being condemned for choosing isolation, there are many successful 'loners' who have contributed significantly to making the world a better place. Notably, many attribute their successes to their isolation as devoting time to thinking and reading without the noise, interruptions and disturbance of others has led to their eureka moments and development of creative ideas. Certainly, it's easier to devour knowledge in books, collect your own thoughts and ponder on subsequent ideas, without the distraction of other people.

From Sir Isaac Newton, who enjoyed alone time and privacy, to Albert Einstein, who developed the theory of relativity, many a creative genius might opt to enjoy the honjok lifestyle today. Said Einstein, 'Be a loner. That gives you time to wonder, to search for the truth. Have holy curiosity. Make your life worth living.' While Pablo Picasso famously stated, 'Without great solitude, no serious work is possible.'

'Without great solitude,
no serious work is possible.'
— PICASSO

DEFINING ALONENESS FOR YOU

While some creative thinkers might seek out solitude so they may focus and generate their best work, not all creative thinkers will. Just as some extroverts, while thriving amid a crowd of people, may not enjoy being around others *all* of the time. Indeed, the traits of our human nature exist on a spectrum, including introversion and extroversion. Even the quietest introvert and most gregarious extrovert are not so inclined 100 per cent of the time.

Perhaps the greatest consideration then is how we each, as individuals, *feel* about being alone.

HOW DOES BEING ALONE MAKE YOU FEEL?

Consider the following questions about how being alone affects you:

- Do you feel pain or glory at the prospect of being alone?

● Does being alone make you feel free to be yourself, away from the restrictions, compromises and limitations that having to consider others can create? Or does it make you feel fearful, lonely, unlovable and unworthy of company?

● Does it make you feel relaxed and happy or anxious and unnerved?

● What degree of aloneness is okay for you? How much alone time do you want (or need) per day? Perhaps you're comfortable being alone, but not for too long. In which case, how long is too long? Perhaps you don't mind spending a few evenings alone, as long as you can talk to people on the phone or via messengers and social media.

● How often do you like to socialize? Is it important for you to interact face-to-face with people every day or are you happy to go a few days or longer without much direct social connection?

DEPENDENCE

One way of defining how aloneness works for you is to consider whether you are generally more dependent, independent or interdependent? Are you reliant on the help of other people? Have you grown dependent on having company? Do you tend to prioritize your own needs or those of others? Perhaps you need to feel needed?

If the latter is true, you may have some co-dependent tendencies, which can impact how you feel about being on your own when there is nobody around to need you. If you feel guilty about being alone because you think you might be needed elsewhere, remind yourself you are not abandoning anyone to spend time on your own, rather you might be liberating them.

Dependency on other people can be as a result of boredom, from not knowing how to entertain yourself. It could also be that you feel safer when you're with other people as you can escape anxiety or a lack of self-worth. As a result, you may find yourself seeking validation and approval from others and feel unable to give yourself the self-approval you deserve.

Perhaps you've spent so long in the company of others that doing so is now habitual. This is not uncommon. And while not knowing how to be on your own can be challenging at first, it is readily overcome by taking small steps and devoting 10–20 minutes each day to being alone, filling the time with enjoyable activities.

The more time you spend being alone without feeling lonely, the more your mindset will shift; you'll rewire your neural pathways and belief systems to see alone time as a positive experience rather than a negative one.

INDEPENDENCE AND INTERDEPENDENCE

Maybe you're reluctant to accept help from others. Perhaps asking for help makes you feel less capable in some way. If so, remember, asking for help or advice is not a weakness. Everyone needs help occasionally and most people like to give advice and help others, especially when asked.

Or perhaps you are more interdependent, meaning you cooperate well with others. All of us are interdependent to a certain degree, even honjoks. We all depend on others to provide running water and food to buy. As children, we need other people to help us learn how to live, so we're dependent on our parents until we gain our own financial and psychological independence. In this way we are all interconnected and reliant on other people to provide the food and products which sustain us.

Only if we become completely self-sufficient and grow our own food, plumb our own water systems and learn to live without any human contact can we remove ourselves from the interdependent world to become entirely independent of others. Yet that would be extreme and honjok living is not about creating a hermit lifestyle with no human contact.

Rather, honjok lifestyle is about choosing to rewrite the rules and disavow societal expectations of marriage, work, and family; instead choosing self-fulfilment and individualism so you may live your own life to the fullest without restriction or compromise that living with others creates.

LIVING A SINGLE LIFE

Another consideration about how aloneness affects us is considering the practical side.

For example, finance, travel, and eating out are activities often set up for couples and families. Meanwhile, navigating parties can also be tricky if you're on your own. Perhaps you feel as if you will constantly face friends matchmaking you with other single people if you attend social gatherings alone. If so, you could have a 'go-to' friend who'll join you in such circumstances, or let the party organizer know you're happy as you are.

Being aware of how you feel about the situations you might face when you go out and about on your own is important to make the most of a honjok lifestyle. Thankfully, in South Korea and other parts of the world, honjok culture is growing so significantly that restaurants are allocating increasing numbers of single-seat tables providing more options for those going solo.

THE SPECTRUM OF INTROVERSION AND EXTROVERSION

While it's true that many introverts prefer to be by themselves, this preference is not exclusive to them. Introverts do not hold a monopoly on enjoying alone time, just as enjoying being with people is not exclusive to extroverts. Introverts enjoy the company of others too; they just tend to prefer smaller groups and closer connections, rather than the company of anyone and everyone. Some introverts are thoughtful and introspective; some are restrained in social situations. Evidently, there is no one-size-fits-all definition. For example, you might be an extrovert who loves being the centre of attention, yet feel compelled to take yourself off to be by yourself at regular intervals.

According to Dan McAdams, PhD, Professor of Psychology and Human Development and Social Policy at Northwestern University, 'Extroversion/ introversion is a continuous dimension, like height and weight. There are people who score at the extremes, like very heavy people, or very tall people, or people who score very high on the trait of extroversion – but most people fall in the middle of these bell-shaped curves.'

Bold and outgoing extroverts tend to relish engaging in a busy and varied social life and being the centre of attention. Conversely, introverts tend to be more reserved, quiet and deliberative, devoting their time to being alone or among smaller groups of close friends. Ambiverts fall somewhere in between, in the centre of the spectrum, and their social flexibility means they're equally comfortable with or without people around them and balance listening with talking.

Ambiverts may have less of a preference towards performing tasks alone or in a group, or they may lean slightly towards one or the other, so while they feel comfortable in most social settings, even busy highly-populated ones, they might feel drained after being around people constantly and seek frequent solitude as a way to recharge. They quite enjoy the occasional feeling of being the centre of attention, but not for too long.

But there is so much more to introversion than being shy or choosing solitariness. In fact, only one type of introversion relates to shyness, and that's the type where anxiety and a sense of awkwardness drive the preference for solitude or small social groups. The other types of introversion range from reserved people who operate at a slower pace to thoughtful introspective day-dreamers, but their tendencies and preferences are not fixed.

Susan Cain, American author of the bestseller *Quiet: The Power of Introverts in a World That Can't Stop Talking*, described the difference between extroverts and introverts in a 2012 TED Talk: '[Introversion] is different from being shy. Shyness is about fear of social judgement. Introversion is more about, how do you respond to stimulation, including social stimulation. Extroverts crave large amounts of stimulation, whereas introverts feel at their most alive, switched-on and capable when they're in quieter, more low-key environments. Not all the time – these things aren't absolute – but a lot of the time.' But first we need to know and understand what zone of stimulation is right for us.

It's useful to know your own temperament; where you fit on the introvert/extrovert spectrum and how much stimulation you need, so you can energize rather than deplete yourself. Those embracing the honjok lifestyle already know that spending time alone energizes them. Now it's your turn to discover what your personality reveals about the level of aloneness you need.

ARE YOU AN INTROVERT, EXTROVERT OR AMBIVERT?

Find out where you fall on the introvert-extrovert spectrum.

When talking to people you don't know, do you feel:
A. Awkward.
B. Energized.
C. It depends on the people.

Do you recharge your batteries best by:
A. Grabbing some alone time.
B. Socializing with a group of friends and/or strangers.
C. Balancing time alone with time with close friends.

When do you find you are most productive?
A. Working in a quiet and peaceful space on your own.
B. Working in a busy cafe or office; you need stimulation.
C. You can be productive in both environments.

Would those closest to you say you are:
A. Quiet and reserved.
B. Outgoing and chatty.
C. Sometimes outgoing but can be quiet too.

If you are out socializing, would you rather spend your time:

A. Connecting in deep conversation with one good friend.

B. Chatting and mingling with a group of people, including strangers (friends you haven't met yet).

C. It depends on your mood but ideally a bit of both.

When communicating with someone new do you tend to:

A. Talk the most.

B. Listen the most.

C. Balance talking and listening relatively equally.

When surrounded by other people, would you rather:

A. Blend into the background.

B. Be in the spotlight.

C. You are comfortable being the centre of attention but not for too long.

Would you rather immerse yourself in:

A. A good book.

B. A good movie.

C. It depends on your mood but you like books and movies.

After spending time surrounded by other people in a noisy and busy atmosphere, do you feel:

A. Drained and invisible.

B. Energized and invincible.

C. Mostly energized, but drained if it's for too long.

When making decisions are you:

A. Cautious.

B. A risk-taker.

C. You spend time weighing the pros and cons but are happy to take informed risks.

At the end of the week do you tend to feel:

A. Understimulated and bored.

B. Overstimulated and overwhelmed.

C. It depends on the kind of week you've had.

When surrounded by other people do you tend to:

A. Observe and listen.

B. Lead and start conversations.

C. Join in.

Do you prefer to:

A. Have some time to daydream.

B. Be busy and active.

C. Do a bit of both.

When it comes to asserting yourself in social situations, do you find it:

A. Difficult.

B. Easy.

C. It depends on the situation.

Does being alone:

A. Energize you.

B. Bore you? Or make you feel like you're missing out.

C. Mostly energizes you.

If you answered mostly As,
you lean towards introversion.
If you answered mostly Bs,
you lean towards extroversion.
If you answered mostly Cs,
you lean towards ambiversion.
If you answered a combination of As, Bs and Cs,
you are most likely an ambivert.

Wherever you fall on the spectrum is perfectly okay. It's how you use this information to inform your choices about alone time and social time which matters most.

DOPAMINE STIMULATION

Our feel-good hormone, dopamine, is partially responsible for how social we are and how being alone makes us feel. Those who have naturally high levels of dopamine-fuelled stimulation of the neocortex (the part of our brain responsible for conscious thought and language) tend to avoid further, and thus overwhelming, stimulation.

On the other hand, those with lower levels might exhibit more extrovert tendencies because feeling under-stimulated causes boredom, which means they need and seek extra stimulation via social interaction in order to generate more dopamine and feel good. For extroverts, in order to balance out your feel-good chemicals, participate in other activities that dish out the dopamine.

WORKING WITH YOUR OWN TEMPERAMENT

Remember, all of us have to be alone at times. For those of you who are extroverts, it may be especially difficult to pull yourself away from others for solitude. You naturally need people to feel energized, and that's okay. For those of you who gain more energy from being alone, it is probably easier to spend time by yourself. You might feel more challenged during the occasions when you're required to be social, and that's okay too. Be kind with yourself about that.

Wherever you find yourself on the introvert/extrovert scale, some of these considerations may be helpful in working with your own temperament.

- Pay attention to how your body feels before and after social events so you can learn more about what you truly need. Tune into your body and become aware of how you're holding yourself – are your shoulders and neck tight? Do you feel constricted? This will help you learn how to cultivate inner calm.

- Consider how you can strengthen your internal side before and after spending time with people. Perhaps play music that helps you feel strong or reflect in a meditation before going out.

● Choose nurturing activities that soothe you to follow social activities that deplete you, like taking a bath, lighting a candle, sitting under a tree or reading a book – anything that honours the part of you that needs to return to a calmer place. By taking deliberate action to calm your nervous system, you're developing a greater awareness of your nature and needs.

● If being alone is a struggle, start your alone time slowly, maybe for a few minutes at a time, and build your tolerance over time. Practice solitude with conscious awareness so you can train yourself how to feel comfortable at those times when you have no choice but to be alone. It may take practice to figure out what works best to bring ease into your body and mind. You could combine it with a tactile experience such as writing or art.

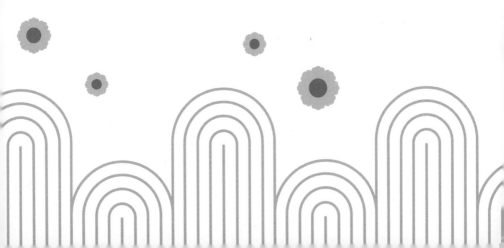

● Cultivate the idea of being your own friend, so when you're alone when you'd rather not be, you still feel okay. Consider ways to look after yourself, especially if you're someone who needs to feel needed. Remind yourself that you need yourself too and cherish moments of self-care during alone time.

● Spend any social time you do have with those you feel a deeper connection with; people who truly see and hear and appreciate you. This will be especially helpful if you tend to feel lonely even in the company of others. Consider how you might develop those deeper connections. If nobody you know fits that criteria, consider joining groups – local or online – which include people who share your interests.

THE NEED TO BELONG

Connections are important because we are, as humans, inherently tribal. Feeling like we belong is an integral human need while supportive relationships have been defined by psychologists as vital for our wellbeing. Notably though, one or two significant relationships can be enough. What's most important is the quality of our relationships, not the quantity.

DEVELOPING DEEPER CONNECTIONS

It's a myth to believe that anyone who enjoys their own company and lives a single lifestyle must be deficient in maintaining strong relationships. In fact, the converse is often true. Those who live honjok lives say their relationships became deeper and more authentic after spending quality time alone. And it makes sense. When you devote sufficient time to being alone, you are better able to tune into your own thoughts and feelings and hone your listening abilities. This combination of supercharged self-knowledge and self-awareness, coupled with fine-tuned listening and empathy skills, can build a strong foundation for deeper connections. What's more, the more awareness you have about who you are and what you want from life, the better you become at knowing who feels most aligned to you.

THE RIGHT CONNECTIONS

Support is a key component of wellbeing, but it's important to choose the right people, those who make you feel held rather than lonely. Sometimes we may feel loneliness when our connections are counterfeit, based on superficial factors like appearance, age or achievements, rather than connecting to the depth of who we are and what never changes about us.

Consider the way people present their lives through their social media feeds. We see polished images of smiling families and beautiful vacation pictures. We develop our own story about who we are through our posted images. It keeps us safe and separate, under the illusion of connection. But what if we focused our attention on deeper connections with those who really see and hear us; those who we feel more of a connection with?

Not all relationships are created equal. Some are supportive, nourishing and encouraging, enabling you to thrive, while others are destructive, stressful, numbing and discouraging. Perhaps because the source of so much stress and frustration comes from the latter kind this is one of the factors that leads people towards a honjok lifestyle.

OPTIMIZING SUPPORTIVE RELATIONSHIPS

Look at the relationships in your life and think about whether they feed or deplete you. Sometimes we're so focused on our history and loyalty that we ignore our wellbeing in relationships. Remember, our early attachments are based only on survival, rather than on nurturing: when you take time to contemplate, you can become honest about your relationships – which ones nourish you and which ones deplete. It may mean we let people go.

❊   Schedule quality time with people who lift you up rather than those who bring you down. Consider what you can do to help deepen those cherished connections, whether it's sending notes and gifts in the mail to organizing to experience something that you'll mutually appreciate, such as joining an evening art class or walking in nature together.

❊   Learn to listen well. Give your full attention, maintain eye contact, ask questions and show an interest. When people share their good news with you, invite them to relive their experience. When they share their bad news with you, nod and practice empathy.

'I exist as I am and that is enough.'
— WALT WHITMAN

YOUR MOST IMPORTANT RELATIONSHIP

As social creatures, our evolution has depended on us living and working together in tribes. Yet, now that the number of honjoks is growing so rapidly, if you choose to pursue this solo lifestyle, you can now take comfort from the fact that as a honjok, you are part of a tribe of people who enjoy their own company and choose to live much of life alone. You belong to the honjok tribe. Perhaps that's enough.

In Japan, where the equivalent of honjok is called 'ohitorisama', businesses have tweaked their offerings to suit the rising trend with karaoke chains and restaurants offering small solo booths after realizing many customers come in on their own. Some bars have even gone as far as to become 'solo only' bars, cultivating a tribe of one.

We all understand what it means to belong to a group, perhaps to our family, friends or a team, and the need to belong and build relationships with people is a fundamental part of human nature. We are social beings. However, the tribes or groups that we become part of can be temporary or transitory. People will come and go in our lives. The most intimate, constant and enduring relationship is the one you have with yourself.

SOLOGAMY

Not all relationships last. But the one with yourself will always exist. So it's worth cherishing that relationship, even celebrating it. That's what sologamy or 'self-marriage' is all about. Sologamy, although not legally recognized, is the act of marrying yourself. Vows are about self-respect, self-belief and self-compassion, and the ritual can be carried out alone or surrounded by friends and family, akin to more traditional wedding ceremonies.

For many it's simply about saying 'yes' to yourself – a celebration of accepting who you are with compassion; a symbolic service of commitment to oneself which proudly declares that you are enough as you are, on your own.

Self-marriage, as an act of self-love, is about treasuring yourself. It's a reminder that you can find fulfilment and live a meaningful life outside of romantic relationships. But it's not a narcissistic act; conversely, the more you are able to show love to yourself, the better equipped you become to accept, love and understand others. Says Sophie Tanner, author of *Reader, I Married Me*, who wed herself in 2015 as a 'commitment to self-compassion': 'Developing a sense of self-worth, as opposed to insecurity, allows even greater capacity for human connection.'

While some sologamists have disconnected from dating, stopped searching for their soulmate and, instead, focus their attention and energy on what fulfils them as individuals, others are simply affirming their wholeness in the absence of another.

At the heart of sologamy is the recognition that it's entirely possible to be completely happy on your own, but it doesn't necessarily mean that you are vowing to forsake all others. Moreover it's about setting a standard about what constitutes a happy relationship and affirming your own value – as an individual, as honjoks do.

Sologamy aside, we can all gain a deeper sense of fulfilment if we embrace the concept of belonging to ourselves, a way of being that we can only achieve if we dedicate time to ourselves for contemplation.

This is a process, and you may experience challenges along the way, from life's distractions to your commitment to exploring your inner world. But it's time well spent.

What's key is moving our mindset away from associating alone time as lacking in some way, from being 'without' other people, and towards being 'with' ourselves, so as fulfilling rather than lacking.

3

THE ART OF
AWARENESS

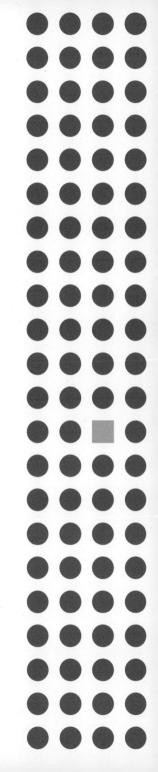

THINKING TIME

When you are alone you get to be with your thoughts and listen to them. We have all our answers inside us already. It's just a case of tuning in and hearing ourselves. Consequently, alone time offers space and thinking time to develop self-awareness. Thinking time helps us to:

- Tap into our intuition and truth so we may make better decisions.

- Meditate and find answers to our most pressing questions.

- Get to know who we are and what we need in order to thrive.

Alone time also allows us to explore and notice our own patterns of behaviour – how we react and respond to situations and figure out ways to adjust our behaviour and respond better. In this way, alone time can be a useful self-improvement tool. Furthermore, it can fertilize the seeds of our ideas and enable us to grow.

This contemplative lifestyle is one of the gifts of
honjok – taking back our power and redefining what
is important to us as individuals.

TIME WELL SPENT

Walden, Galileo, Socrates, Thoreau, and many others understood the value of contemplative time. Think about some of the great Buddhists – the Dalai Lama, Pema Chödrön and Thich Nhat Hanh – and the works they produced from their contemplative time.

Contrary to the notion of contemplative moments being a waste of time, investing in self-reflection to develop self-awareness and compassion actually helps you save time by gaining a better understanding of what matters most so you can invest time in those areas. You get to decide at what level you want to be involved in the world, at what point you lose yourself, and where the balance is.

How often are we lost in the external expectations around us? When are we saying 'Yes' when we mean 'No'? How do we direct our time? The art of awareness gives us the power back to direct it where we'll gain the best return on our investment.

Devoting alone time to these questions brings in a consciousness around how you feed your energy and time. You're not just running around checking items off to-do lists. You are a leader of your own domain and life. The tasks aren't leading you. You're leading the tasks; making choices deliberately and shaping your life consciously and independently. Are you ready to get back in the driving seat of your life?

'I love to be alone. I never found the companion that was so companionable as solitude.'
— HENRY DAVID THOREAU

TRUE SELF VS FALSE SELF

Building a caring relationship with yourself is an empowering action and a foundational step towards wholeness. Because, within a kind and loving relationship, the true self naturally emerges.

You no longer need to continue with patterns and responses, which no longer serve you, just to suit others – something at the very heart of honjok life. You no longer need to abide by societal, cultural and gender-based expectations and stereotypes.

Now, all that matters is what matters most to *you* as an individual, not what matters most to society. You can stop being dictated to, explore what your heart desires and follow what your true self dictates. This is the value of self-reflection and building a practice of contemplation.

You can be your authentic self, rather than living a life where your energy is drained as you try to be who you think you ought to be, rather than who you truly are. This is the value of honjok.

In her book, *Quiet*, Susan Cain encourages us to nurture our natures: 'Stay true to your own nature. If you like to do things in a slow and steady way, don't let others make you feel as if you have to race. If you enjoy depth, don't force yourself to seek breadth. If you prefer single-tasking to multi-tasking, stick to your guns. Being relatively unmoved by rewards gives you the incalculable power to go your own way.'

'Having learned the ways of silence
within the noise of urban life
I take life as it comes to me
And everywhere I am is true.'
— MATSUO BASHO

GREAT EXPECTATIONS

Becoming an expert on you is empowering but doesn't mean completely dismissing other points of view and feedback. It means knowing and voicing your truth, even if it is unpopular. Too easily we sign over our voice to cooperate with the idea of what is expected of us. Just because it works for another does not mean it will work for you.

While it's important to be aware of societal 'shoulds', it's more crucial to be aware and accepting of who we truly are. Just as we hand over our power to others' expectations about who we should be, we may also hand over our power to how we should present ourselves in relation to others.

Think about the social media culture and how people post the best of themselves and leave out the worst. These are not authentic representations. The true authentic self is not on display here. Yet we feel inadequate in response. We compare and despair. So how can we counter this?

We do this by developing self-awareness and self-acceptance. Only when you feel strong and secure in who you are will you stop yourself being weakened by other peoples' strengths. Such resilience equips you to respond to life's challenges with faith and fluidity rather than restriction and fear.

GETTING TO KNOW YOU

Given that the most constant and enduring relationship we have in life is the one we have with ourselves, it makes sense to get to know who we are as best we can.

By being alone, we get to give ourselves the attention we deserve. Through self-reflection we are able to respond to ourselves the way we may have always wished others would respond to us. As we become increasingly self-aware, we become conscious of our motivations, impulses, insecurities, needs, feelings, desires, passions and concerns, which often evolve over time, and so require continued attention. By doing so we can respond with greater care.

INFLUENCED BELIEFS
We each have a set of beliefs about who we are, our characteristics and preferences, our flaws and strengths. We've formed these beliefs based on what we've learned from our direct experiences in the world. Our families, cultural influences and societal expectations have also shaped us.

Unfortunately, we often adopt these beliefs about ourselves without questioning whether they are wholly accurate. Perhaps you've pursued a career that was expected of you without considering whether the profession sparked joy in you. Maybe you attend lots of parties because your family always prioritized social activities. You may feel overextended but don't reflect on whether constantly surrounding yourself with others is actually important to you. So how do we know our beliefs are true? Do we truly understand who we are, absent of any other influence? There's only one way to find out and that's to spend time alone cultivating self-awareness.

SELF-REFLECTION

Questioning your beliefs and listening for answers within yourself requires time alone in contemplation and the courage to question what you've been taught. Through this process of self-reflection you can:

- Ask yourself which beliefs have come from external authors of your story, rather than from your true self and take time to reframe them to be more accurate.

- Discover your deeper goals and passions to understand what sparks joy in you.

- Find your forte and realize your strengths.

- Hear and honour your intuition to make decisions that resonate with your truth.

- Try to gain a deeper understanding of what matters most to you.

- Lean into your feelings to gain insight into your deeper self.

- Notice behavioural patterns and responses and work on shifting those that don't serve you.

WHO ARE YOU?

* ✳ What makes you, you? What are your strengths and weaknesses?

* ✳ What strengths do you wish to nurture?

* ✳ List the 'shoulds' and expectations you sometimes feel pressurized by.

* ✳ How do these fit (or not) with how you want to show up in the world? Do they match your true self?

* ✳ What are your beliefs and values?

* ✳ What triggers you to react negatively?

* ✳ What patterns of behaviour and tendencies do you notice?

'If you are never alone,
you cannot know yourself.'
— PAULO COELHO

WHAT DO YOU WANT AND NEED?

Knowing how you want to feel and what you want from life provides potent clarity.

It can be hard to work out what your needs are. It is sometimes difficult to differentiate between your needs and the expectations of others. Only when you consciously carve out time in your schedule to be alone with your thoughts can you learn what you need: perhaps that having more quiet in your life and time alone to contemplate the life you want might allow space for your creativity to flourish.

This book is an invitation to shift your perspective towards one where you matter enough to consider your needs. When you give as much importance to your inner world as you do to work and external influences, you can develop a better understanding of who you are and thrive accordingly.

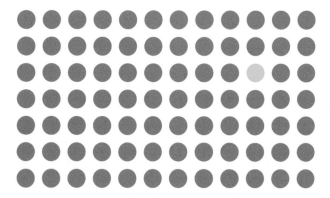

The honjok lifestyle gives you time alone to explore your own needs, to uncover what matters most and why so. So, let's find out:

1. Create a serenity space for deep listening in solitude. This could be a quiet corner of a room with a comfortable chair or beanbag, comfy cushions and hot cup of tea, notepad and book. Or perhaps you favour being out in nature and your serenity space is under a big tree.

2. Ask yourself the following questions, take a few long deep breaths and listen to your answers.

    ●   What's your spark? What do you enjoy doing so much that you often lose track of time while doing it?

    ●   What matters most to you? If you only had one week left to live, what would you want to do and who with?

    ●   What is it that you are seeking? Belonging? Acceptance? Prosperity? Love? Freedom? We are all wired to think of 'treasure' as something worth getting, and that something is different for everyone.

- How do you wish to feel at the end of each day?

- What activities make you feel this way?

- How might you spend more time on these activities and less time on those which you feel drain you?

- What gives your life meaning and purpose?

Reflecting on your answers, what actions do you want to take? What do you want to work on and what do you want to celebrate? What do you want to do more and less of?

NOTICING HOW YOU FEEL

Staying present and tuning into our feelings gives us insight into our deeper selves. It can also help us to process past hurts, to grieve and then grow, as we learn important lessons that we can take forwards.

FEELING INTO FEELING

Empathy builds when we acknowledge the feeling that is present without judging it as bad or wrong or trying to fix or solve it.

Rather than pushing away any emotion we perceive to be negative or bury it deep inside, we can use our alone time to move from suppression (which can cause depression) to expression. By releasing our emotions and letting them flow, we can work through them and move forwards.

1. Allow the feeling to be present and give yourself permission to have this human response.

2. Notice how your body feels and pay attention to its sensations. Bodily discomfort is often a sign to

pay attention to something that needs tweaking, rather than a sign we need to take painkillers and continue doing what we've always done.

3. Label feelings as you express them. Say, 'I feel sad ...' or 'This has made me feel angry ...'. Labelling feelings has been proven to take the power away from them and help us work our way through them faster.

4. Ask yourself: 'What do I need today?' Perhaps a cup of tea, a call with a friend or a walk in nature would help. Perhaps jotting down a plan of action, solution to a problem, lessons learned or ways to change would feel more proactive. Or perhaps simply sitting with and leaning into your feelings is help enough.

5. Congratulate yourself for taking time to listen and hear what your feelings are telling you. They are giving you an early-warning system that something might need to change. As a result, the guidance you receive from your self-inquiry could lead you in a new and inspiring direction. Or, perhaps the simple awareness that something does need to change (even if you don't know what that is just yet) is enough for now. The good news is you are listening now. We need only foster our capacity to listen and hear the underlying message.

CULTiVATiNG A CURiOUS MiND

Building skills to self-reflect with compassion and curiosity, rather than criticism and judgement, sets a trusting precedent with ourselves which reinforces the self-reciprocity inherent in listening to our bodies, emotions, and thoughts with respect and then responding accordingly.

CURIOSITY VS JUDGEMENT

Many people who call themselves honjoks work on cultivating a curious mind. This provides a counterpart to the judge who lives inside us all. It's about allowing yourself to be open-minded about who you are by letting go of any preconceived judgements about what is good or bad.

We all face judgement on many aspects of our lives – our choices, appearance, lifestyle, career or socio-economic status.

Exploring who we are with curiosity rather than criticism invites us to use discernment about our choices, while respecting ourselves and other people's individual paths, so we may ask ourselves who we might be if we had no fear of others' judgement.

This is an invitation to explore these questions, honour your curiosity and be true to yourself and your intuition. First, you discover your nature without judging it, then you figure out how to work with it.

REAL-TIME CURIOSITY

Being curious about your feelings, thoughts, and behaviour gives you the space to consider what they might be showing you, as opposed to critiquing them.

- Pause throughout the day to check in with how you feel mentally, physically and emotionally.

- Notice with curiosity throughout the day in real time and during some intentional reflection time at the end of the day. Pay attention to which activities, comments, conversations and ruminations energize you and which drain you. Which cause you distress, unease or anxiety and which make you feel valued, peaceful or at ease? This is how you learn about what truly resonates with you and what may cause you harm.

- Without judgement, consider what you could do differently to support yourself. How might you avoid situations, conversations or activities which deplete your nature and how might you devote more time to those which align?

Stay curious and open. The curious mind requires mindful attunement to our inner world and experience. When we cultivate this practice we can build the muscle of inquiry.

LIVING ACCORDING TO YOUR NEEDS

It takes courage to be honest about what you need. Sometimes our beliefs and judgements interfere with our ability to identify our needs and consider them valid, or our needs become distorted by our concern for meeting other people's needs. Transcend your judgemental mind and be curious about yourself.

We may believe our needs are too much or a burden to others. Think about how we can ask for what we need from ourselves and our relationships. Do we lose sight of our needs because they are overshadowed by the needs of others? Do we deny our need to cry because we feel it's not appropriate?

Once you understand your needs, you can look for ways to care for yourself better. Maybe you cry in the shower or scream in your car. You could consider making your needs more visible to others by starting to share your feelings honestly without seeking any solution. I'm feeling mad at myself today. I'm feeling sad. Rather than pretending you're fine, practice feeling vulnerable.

BEING THE AUTHOR
OF YOUR OWN STORY

We are most powerful when we choose how to frame what happens to us. To do that, we have to spend time alone, cultivating strength to reframe our stories. We all have stories we tell ourselves that shape our behaviour and attitude towards ourselves. These stories are core beliefs that run us. When we don't explore them, we default to them.

For example, we might have stories and beliefs which make it challenging for us to be alone, even though doing so could be exactly what we need. For example, we might tell ourselves:

- Being alone means nobody loves me.

- Happiness comes from a marriage.

- I'm supposed to strive for a partnership.

- If I ask to be alone, it means I'm rejecting others.

It takes courage and risk to get rid of a story and live in a space where you don't know what you believe. When you allow that space and openness, you can discover what you really feel and what is true for you. The story – whether you have made it up or someone gave it to you – could have been a logical conclusion or something that seemed true for a time. You don't have to keep proving that it's true. Questioning and reframing our stories liberates us from the old limitations. You're willing to give up what you think you know in order to discover what you know is true for you now.

THE INNER CRITIC WITHIN US ALL

According to modern psychology, most of our thinking on a daily basis is negative self-talk.

This is due to our built-in negativity bias which used to protect us from being ejected from the tribe and potential danger, back when being a valuable member of a tribe was part of our survival and danger lurked round every corner. However, as we have evolved, our brain no longer needs to focus its attention on negative judgements or concerns. Yet our constant self-talk continues to guide how we feel and make choices every day.

We all have crises of self-worth, especially when we're engaging in a pattern of negative self-talk, condemning ourselves for anything that goes wrong and feeling like a failure if we don't live up to the expectations of our boss or family. It's easy to spiral into a cycle of ruminating over our mistakes, second-guessing our decisions, thereby further fuelling our inadequacies. One of the benefits of being alone is to be able to devote time to tune in to your internal radio station so you can reduce (or at least reframe) such self-talk.

WORKING WITH YOUR INNER CRITIC

- **Sit quietly, with a journal and no distractions.** Without censoring yourself, put your flow of thoughts onto the pages and see what comes up. What are you telling yourself? What do you judge and blame yourself about the most? Needing help? Being untidy? Making mistakes? Not being slim, fit, funny, kind, clever enough? Don't judge yourself – simply consider it as you might a friend's story. We all tell ourselves different stories about who we are, but are they really true? Repeated thoughts can become steadfast beliefs, but they are often inaccurate, fed to us over time by our families, peers, teachers and society at large.

- **Consider what has led you to have this belief.** Why does a particular story exist and why do you believe it? By exploring these negative voices and where they come from, we find that many originate from what others have told us and want us to believe.

- **Take your thoughts to court.** Try to dispute your negative self-talk. Look at each thought and collect evidence for and against it. If there is even one piece of evidence that it may not be true, you can consider stopping those thoughts in their tracks so you can reframe them.

- **Reframe thoughts that could be disputed.** Say, 'What's another way of looking at this?' For example, if your negative self-talk is: 'I'm a terrible friend', having found evidence to the contrary, such as, 'I message my friends as often as they message me', you can reframe the original negative criticism to something more compassionate, such as, 'I'm a good and caring friend. Sometimes we are so busy that we don't see each other. Perhaps we can set up a date to meet at the end of each month.'

- **Let inaccurate beliefs go.** Say out loud each story that you've believed. If you notice an emotional or physical response, say: 'I forgive myself for believing that ... (repeat the belief).' Take a breath. With your exhale, hold the intention that you're releasing this narrative.

- **Remember that you are enough!** You are more than your achievements, skills and experience. Your qualities are important and valuable.

In future, notice when your inner voice is criticizing you, observe those intrusive thoughts and call them out as intruders. In your mind, say, 'Stop!' and return to your curious mind. I wonder why I'm thinking this now? Why am I questioning that choice? Why do I continue to blame myself? Give yourself time to answer. Now recognize them for what they are: your negativity bias critic speaking. These thoughts most likely aren't true. That's not who you are.

By spending time alone in deep contemplation, you are building your inner strength so that you aren't knocked out by inaccurate stories or your inner critic. It takes grit, fortitude and commitment. You also need to develop a tolerance for feeling discomfort; get comfortable with your imperfections, and make yourself vulnerable enough to show those imperfections to the world.

Part of learning who you are is about working your way towards acceptance of all parts of you. As well as turning down the volume on your inner critic and working with that negative self-talk to create more accurate stories, it also involves turning up the volume on your inner encourager, and that takes compassion.

'You cannot be lonely if you like the person you're alone with.'
— WAYNE DYER

BUILDING
SELF-WORTH

What if everything so far in your life has brought you right to this very moment? To the place where you are beginning to consider you are worth more than you thought you were. What if every hardship has been in service to your own awakening into a deeper understanding of yourself? This means you can trust yourself and your life. This also means you can have the courage to spend time alone without interference.

Everything in your life, on the micro and macro levels, is working for you. Every disturbance, irritant and discontent is grist for the mill; a stepping-stone for you to reach deeper into yourself than ever before, past all the pressure and judgements and attachments. The world is for your own liberation. Liberation is the opposite of control. Beyond liberation lies peace. But we can only invite such peace into our lives when we feel we are worthy. Building our capacity for compassion helps us achieve this sense of calm acceptance.

Through self-acceptance and self-compassion we can free ourselves from other people's opinions, validation and approval.

CULTIVATING COMPASSION

Alone time gives us the opportunity to give ourselves permission to be human. We can remind ourselves that we don't have to have this all figured out. We only need to listen to ourselves and become our own best friend, giving ourselves the support we need.

Some people choose distractions – from alcohol and drugs to shopping and television – as a way to counter their harsh critic. They choose to numb rather than nourish themselves; to escape rather than connect. Yet distractions are only temporary fixes.

BEFRIEND YOURSELF

When we become our own best friend, we free ourselves from other people's opinions and approval. We become more willing to trust ourselves, rather than relying on others to make us feel good.

Inner approval, as opposed to external approval or permission from others, can be one of the most radically empowering strategies you can deploy. Instead of wishing that they understand you, love you, appreciate you, see how good you are, or recognize your value, why not do this for yourself?

- Instead of turning to something to numb you, try sitting with your pain as a compassionate observer, reminding yourself that feelings come and go. Have compassion for yourself for living with those feelings. Talk to yourself as you would a friend who's struggling.

- Consider what message you would long to hear from another. Is there someone in your life you wished had said, 'I love you', or 'I'm so proud of you', or 'I believe in you'? What if you started saying this to yourself on a daily basis, whenever you felt you needed to hear it, as often as you like?

Being willing to do this requires that we let go of controlling another person and needing someone else to show up a certain way in order for us to be okay. We take back our power this way. Fortunately, through doing this simple activity, we prove to ourselves that we really are in charge of how we feel.

One of the biggest obstacles people face when they make changes in their lives is the concern about what others might think and if they might be judged or rejected in some way. But if we consistently give ourselves approval, allow ourselves permission to be imperfectly human and, in doing so, accept ourselves, we are no longer tied to another's approval. We are free to move towards and make changes regardless of what others think. This is central to the honjok mindset.

When we give ourselves the inner approval we need to make our changes, it becomes easier to allow others their reactions. Such inner strength isn't determined by accolades or criticism, it's a sense of staying steady. Your wellbeing is not contingent on the company of others because they cannot define who you are better than youself can.

COMPASSIONATE ACTION

- Ask yourself: if my job, money, family and health were taken away, what would be left that doesn't change? This is cultivating self-worth.

- Building on the knowledge you've gained about who you are as a result of self-reflection during alone time, ask: what is the music of your nature? What is right with you? This shifts attention away from our default negativity bias-led focus of what is wrong with you.

- Commit to using your character strengths on a regular basis. According to the founder of positive psychology, Professor Martin Seligman, deploying our gifts, such as kindness, creativity, hope and gratitude, on a regular basis has a direct impact on our level of wellbeing and life satisfaction.

- Assess what your social media use does to your own self-worth. So many of us use social media as a way to connect, to buffer ourselves from feeling lonely, yet our worth crumbles when we don't get enough likes. However, social media is not a forum for being vulnerable and cultivating meaningful and

deep connections. It may offer you something but be aware of what you are seeking. Are you escaping? Are you constantly checking to see how many likes you've generated? I think you'll find there's more enjoyment to be found being truly present with someone or developing a deep understanding and trust of yourself. If your social media usage is proving detrimental, choose to minimize it.

- Track your progress. Can you accept criticism from your boss or partner without internalizing it as being something that is wrong with you or the quality of your work? Can you view that criticism as an opportunity for betterment, as a chance to grow? Can you accept that you're learning and there's room to make mistakes? Just pivoting and noticing when you're starting to blame yourself is progress.

'The root of true confidence grows from our ability to be in unconditional friendship with ourselves.'
— PEMA CHÖDRÖN

The more we accept ourselves, the more we believe in ourselves. The more self-compassion we give ourselves, the higher our self-esteem. And the better our self-esteem, the more comfortable we'll feel with spending time in our own company, honjok style.

Cultivating self-worth is about preparing for a lifetime where change is inevitable. Our jobs change; our children grow; our parents die; our bodies decline. Our roles of daughter, son, athlete and executive, caretaker – they will all change.

This work of being alone is about investing in that truth. When you begin that investment, the better you can integrate the tides of change that you will face in your life. Change always starts with awareness. And with the art of awareness we can more consciously and intentionally pursue solo activities that resonate best with us and do more of what lights us up, so we may create the feelings we want to feel and the life we hope to lead.

4

ACTS OF SOLITUDE

EMBRACING
ALONE TIME

Honjok life offers an antidote to and relief from the continuous contact of our fast-paced world. It is about the opportunity to escape from the masses. Embracing acts of solitude has the advantage of greater depth and offers a number of benefits: it offers breathing space, autonomy over decisions and the freedom to do as you please, how you please. Pleasure of individualism is, as such, a driving force for the honjok lifestyle.

GOING SOLO

Choosing to live in the present moment for yourself rather than others is central to honjok. Alone time provides the opportunity to focus on the now. It's easier to practice the art of being fully present with minimal distractions. You can pay more attention to what you are doing and the world around you when you are not disturbed by others. You can focus fully on the experience of enjoying your meal or savouring your stroll when nobody is demanding your attention or conversation.

Of course, honjok isn't only about relaxing at home, alone, with nobody else around, it is also about participating in activities solo, even among crowds of others - whether going out for a drink or meal, going to the cinema or travelling solo.

One benefit to honjok living is the ability to save money. Going out with a group of people may mean splitting the cost of a meal or buying rounds of drinks. Dining solo costs less.

Perhaps the biggest benefit of doing such activities on your own is the freedom to choose where you go and what you do without having to consider other peoples' needs, wishes or dietary requirements. You can do whatever you like.

This freedom from restriction or limitation is a key attraction of the honjok lifestyle. You can constantly consider what is pleasurable rather than rational and please yourself instead of others.

JOMO

Fear of loneliness and FOMO (Fear of Missing Out) can prevent us from taking time for ourselves. But what about the Joy of Missing Out? This is when we celebrate a cancelled event or decide not to attend something social and instead prioritize alone time. It provides the opportunity to do whatever we choose. Instead of getting ourselves spruced up, we can enjoy wearing our comfortable clothes and the cosiness of an unplanned night in.

THE JOY OF AUTHENTICITY

In addition to the freedom of autonomy and choice, honjok life provides the freedom to just be yourself, without having to pander to expectations or change who you are to fit in.

Alone time gives us the chance to remove our masks and brave-faced smiles and be our authentic selves. When there is nobody else around, we can bare our true souls. We don't need to pretend, we get to just be.

Consequently, one of the most impactful things we can do for ourselves is create space for rest in solitude without trying to do anything or be something. Simply allowing the mystery of what unfolds to be present, so we can let go of all the 'shoulds' that life sends our way. We can be still and lean into who we are without judgement.

In this way, aloneness can generate a sense of loving acceptance of yourself; a feeling that you are enough.

MORE ME-TIME

As well as costing less money, eating and drinking alone takes up less time. We don't need to drive to someone's house to pick them up *en route* to a restaurant or spend time catching up before we order or after we eat. Meanwhile, honjoks get to invest the time they save spent with others on themselves.

This is useful. Especially given that the busyness and intensity of everyday life has created a sense of time scarcity. This has led to a keenness to make the most of each moment.

Work pressures and after-work social obligations amplify this time scarcity and the incessant need to keep up. The constant distractions of everyday life keep us from connecting properly with each other and ourselves. We tune out rather than in as we focus our attention on ploughing through to-do lists.

Honjok life provides the gift of more me-time; more time to slow down and pause; an opportunity for serenity. We can choose to fill that time with pleasurable activities, such as reading, drawing or singing. Or we can devote that time to simply doing nothing and tuning in to ourselves; honouring our thoughts and our feelings.

Whether you read, meditate, cook, garden, create, fantasize; write, play or listen to music, sit, sunbathe or just bathe, there are so many ways to embrace alone time and make it work for you.

CREATING
SELF-CARE RITUALS

If you can create a ritual that defines your alone time, such as drinking a cup of tea or sitting in a particular place, it will help you turn it into a habit rather than a luxury.

Try and schedule self-care as you would any other appointment in your calendar. You are having an appointment with yourself, which is just as vital, possibly more so, than any other.

You might squeeze in moments as you transition from your work day to home life, or first thing in the morning. The more you ritualize these, the more habitual and therefore sustainable they'll become.

Listen to yourself and ask, 'What do I need today?' Choose to nourish rather than numb yourself and, where possible, make your self-care rituals habitual.

Create a serenity space to cultivate deep listening in solitude. What props could help you better savour your self-care and alone time? A quiet corner of a room with a comfortable cushion and a hot cup of tea? A bench under your favourite tree? Your favourite book? A sketch pad? A journal?

SELF-CARE RITUALS

- A relaxing bath filled with your favourite oils or a refreshing shower.

- Walking in nature or a morning swim.

- Choosing to read or relax rather than zone out to Netflix.

- Devotion to creative play such as drawing, painting, colouring or crafting.

- Having a regular massage, facial or spa day.

- Napping or dancing, whatever it is you need in that moment.

- Showing yourself love by listing everything you like about yourself.

- Journalling or meditation.

- Making yourself a warming cup of herbal tea, wrapping yourself in a blanket and sitting in a comfortable place with your thoughts.

SELF-REFLECTION
AND JOURNALLING

Journal writing isn't something to do just for posterity, the benefits of jotting down thoughts, feelings and concerns in a journal are many. There's personal power in putting pen to paper as you can process emotions, achieve goals, increase self-awareness and improve emotional intelligence.

Journalling helps process your authenticity and enables you to gain clarity, clear your head and to sleep better and feel better as the act of writing helps you put things into perspective, make sense of jumbled thoughts and find solutions to problems. It can help you to capture precious moments and pay more attention to what's happened in your day and it will enable you to engage more with your thoughts. Through journalling, your time alone can be productive, positive and therapeutic.

You might write:

- Morning pages: made famous by Julia Cameron in her book *The Artist's Way*, morning pages can spark your creativity as you write a few pages of 'stream of consciousness' each and every morning, without thinking about what you're writing. This can bring forward ideas and thoughts you weren't consciously aware of and act as a catalyst for cultivating changes in your life.

- Hopes and plans for the future: these could describe what you hope your life might look like in a year's time, five years' time and ten years' time. Paint a picture and consider what small steps could you take today to get closer to those dreams.

- A gratitude list: this might include what you are grateful for now and in the present moment. Researchers in the field of positive psychology have found a great many benefits to expressing gratitude by recording three or more things you are grateful for. Focusing our attention on what we have, rather than what we don't yet have, boosts positive emotion and bolsters wellbeing. Jot down who or what you're grateful for and why, and record any enjoyable moments you wish to savour. This will also make for positive reading to reminisce on in the future.

- A list of achievements: this can counter any feelings of not being good enough. Reminding yourself about your accomplishments can give you a needed confidence boost about what you're capable of.

- A letter of thanks or apology: you don't have to send this but it might help you to feel better about something that may have happened in the past.

- Concerns, ideas and lists: this can be anything which you wish to get out of your head and onto paper so you can get on with your day.

MEDITATION

Alone time doesn't need to be productive in the traditional sense. Modern society may have created a cellular, deep-seated urge to be productive, one where it's commonplace to tie our productivity to our worth, yet research has shown that the ancient tradition of meditation has benefits that can help rather than hinder our productivity.

Of course, taking time out of our busy schedules to meditate may feel counter-intuitive but doing so has the power to boost our concentration levels and lengthen our attention-span, while at the same time reducing our stress and anxiety levels, so it is a useful tool in helping us focus better during the time we devote to working. Another benefit of meditation is that it enhances self-awareness. So, claim some time to be present with yourself.

First, find a quiet space alone and set your timer for at least ten minutes. You can either sit upright or lie down. Then start by breathing in deeply for a count of five and out for a count of six.

MINDFULNESS MEDITATION

This type of meditation invites you to focus on your senses and your breath.

- Keep your eyes open and list what you notice around you.

- Close your eyes and focus your attention on what you can hear – first focus on what you can hear close by, then tune your attention to what you can hear in the distance.

- Consider what you can smell, taste and touch; use your senses to connect back to yourself.

- Take a slow, deep breath in and out. Feel your body's sensations and list them in your mind.

- Focus your attention back on your breath.

- As thoughts pop into your mind, simply let them float by, without judgement, and bring your attention back to your breath and then to your senses.

- Repeat, what can you see, hear, taste, smell, touch? And then focus back to your breath.

- Say in your head, 'Breathing in, 2, 3, 4,' 'Breathing out, 2, 3, 4,' and pay attention to how your breath feels as it enters and leaves your body. Notice your stomach rise and fall.

- Focus on breathing and bring your mind back to your breath each time it goes elsewhere.

You might prefer to use a prop, such as a candle, and focus on the flame. Allow your mind to grow quiet. Let thoughts wash over you. Don't judge them. Don't hold onto them. If your mind feels too busy, focus on the flame. When your time is up, thank yourself for taking the time to care for yourself.

GUIDED MEDITATION

You might prefer to try guided meditations by installing certain apps. Listen to the words guiding your attention and follow the instructions as you breathe slowly in and out.

Researchers at Harvard University have found that regular mindfulness meditation has the power to positively alter the brain's structure, increasing the cortical thickness of the hippocampus, the part of the brain responsible for memory and learning, so devoting alone time to meditating is a wonderful way to equip yourself to grow and improve.

MEDITATIVE MOVEMENT

Too often we look at movement in our lives as a necessary discipline, a way to follow prescribed health guidelines. We forget about the joy in it. Do you remember how it felt to run as a kid? You didn't think about what your body looked like. You weren't concerned with whether your arms were flapping, and you probably weren't even thinking about your destination. You were simply in the moment, feeling your body's power as your lungs pumped and your legs surged forward. Your mind was connected to your body.

As an adult, it feels harder to drop into that mind-body connection as naturally as children do. It is possible, though, to cultivate this experience through meditative movement, a way of moving that centres and calms you, allows you to connect your mind to your body so you're not thinking about the past or the future. You're not worrying and planning. You simply are. Whether you are attending a class solo but surrounded by people, or are entirely on your own, meditative movement fits well with the honjok lifestyle as it focuses on cultivating that mind-body connection.

A 2018 article published in the *Journal of Clinical Medicine* reported that traditional meditative movements, such as tai chi, yoga and qigong, have been effective in treating issues like anxiety, sleep problems and depression. The combination of stretching, breathing and relaxing through these types of movement have soared in popularity as more people are seeking ways to calm their minds in a busy world. In a recent National Health Interview Survey in the United States, Americans ranked those three activities as their preferred complementary therapies.

But you don't have to do these things to develop a mind-body connection through moving. One of the wonderful aspects of meditative movement is that there is no right or wrong path. You can practice this with any kind of solo physical activity, including working out at a gym or dancing in the centre of a packed club.

Consider how you love to move. Do you derive joy from skipping, leaping in the air, twirling, dancing or speed skating? What kind of physical activity could help you generate a sense of flow, where you lose yourself in the moment? How did you love to move as a child? Do that. Shoot some hoops in your neighbourhood park. Run as fast as you can down your road. Ride your bike alone on a country road. Dance across your lawn with bare feet. Breathe. Don't judge. Don't think of others. Just be.

WALKiNG iN NATURE

Public health researchers have found that spending time in nature offers the restorative power of relieving stress as well as enhancing our physical wellbeing by boosting our immune function and reducing our blood pressure. In 1984, Robert Ulrich, PhD, a professor at Chalmers University of Technology in Sweden, found patients coped with pain better after surgery if they had a view of trees from their windows.

Evidence from more than 140 studies involving 290 million people has also determined that exposure to green space including open, undeveloped land with natural vegetation, city parks and street greenery – gives people a significant health boost.

Across the world, people have embraced nature in a variety of different ways. Forest bathing or *shinrin-yoku* is a popular therapy in Japan, where people spend time in the forest, sitting, lying down or walking. In the Netherlands, people seek out windy exercise, a practice known as *uitwaaien*, which translates as 'outblowing', and serves to clear your mind and refresh you.

When you spend time alone outside walking in nature, you are able to connect to the natural world as you tune into the sights and sounds around you: the wind through the trees, the ripples on a lake, birds tweeting in the branches or the faint whisper of a forest through the lens of wonderment.

Think about a regular route you take each day. When was the last time you truly paid attention during that journey? Commit to being more present and notice what's around you.

- Notice the street signs, the trees along the way. Pay attention to the clouds in the sky, people walking by. Observe how your body feels, how your breath sounds and what thoughts come and go.

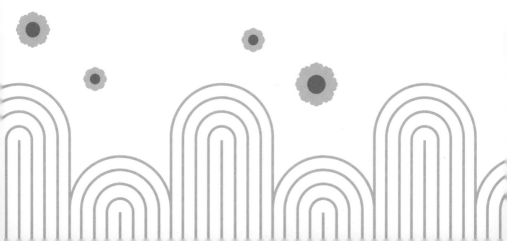

● Walk through woodland or other green space nearby. Sit under a tree and listen with a sense of awe. Watch the palette shift as time passes. Observe the sensations in your body, as the air moves against you, and feel the sweet calm of presence. Notice how quiet spaces calm you. Perhaps go for an evening walk alone under a full moon. Listen. Listen deeply. See how it awakens you.

● Use your senses as you walk to pay attention to everything around you. Consider the sounds you hear, the scenery you see, the smells you encounter, the feel of the ground beneath your feet. Act as if you've never seen or heard or smelled this place before and be curious about what you experience.

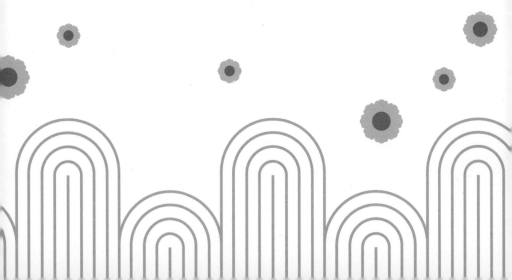

EXPLORING YOUR CREATIVE SIDE

For many years, people have used art therapy as a way to tap into emotions that are too difficult to express in words. You don't need to go to a therapist or find a class to learn how to make art. You don't have to sign up for yet another scheduled activity. This is something you can do on your own. Right now.

Creativity is available to all of us, regardless of our income, age or ability. There is only this rule: set aside your beliefs about yourself. This includes your judgements and views about how creative you are and any desire to be perfect.

This isn't about creating the most perfect piece. It's about taking the time to pause in your busy life, express yourself and stay in the moment. With this in mind, colouring could be the perfect entry into your creativity, especially if you're uncomfortable with the idea of doing something artistic or writing.

There's a reason adult colouring books have become popular in recent years. Colouring sends a signal to our nervous system to be present. It also helps reduce adrenaline and cortisol (stress hormones) in our body.

Perhaps you are more drawn to crafting poems, writing notes to loved ones or making lists and plans for your life. If writing calls to you, it can deepen your intimacy with yourself, with solitude, and with life. Here are some ways to tap into your creativity:

- Schedule creativity – take 10–15 minutes in your day to pause in your work, studies, or social appointments.

- Consider how you can tap into your creativity in a way that can silence your busy mind, and have the relevant tools of creativity on hand, so you can grab them at any time. Invest in a simple set of watercolour paints, brushes and paper or a good camera so you can snap pictures of anything that calls you when you're out and about. Find some writing prompts online and invest in a good notebook and pen.

- See a blank piece of paper as a way to express yourself. Think about what your body wants to show you. You may find that you resolve a challenge you've been facing, or perhaps you can see issues in your life more clearly or you are better able to process something that happened to you.

● Free write, doodle, draw or paint – be open to whatever creative outlet flows through you in that moment. Pick a colour that reflects your emotion. Maybe you'll draw something. Or you could take that time to let your stream of consciousness flow onto the paper through words, without critiquing or polishing. This kind of uninterrupted doodling, painting, writing or colouring allows us to move through our feelings so our bodies don't hold onto difficult emotions.

You don't have to be eloquent or artistic to tap into your creative side. You just have to access your curious mind and let your emotions take the lead. See where they take you. Follow your imagination. Suspend the inner critic. And see what unfolds.

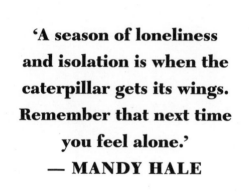

'A season of loneliness
and isolation is when the
caterpillar gets its wings.
Remember that next time
you feel alone.'
— MANDY HALE

SEEKING ADVENTURE

Solo travel has soared in popularity in the last decade. It offers the opportunity to go where you want, when you want and do whatever you want while you're there. For those living a honjok lifestyle, it encapsulates the feeling of freedom gained from living a single life. You make a plan with yourself and off you go.

When travelling by yourself, you can connect with people when you feel like it, and immerse yourself in a book without anyone complaining about your inner focus when you do not. It can be a freeing experience.

Travelling solo offers another opportunity for you to consider what matters most to you as you notice what brings you joy in your day. That might be successfully finding your way around a new town or having conversations with people you meet at a local tavern. Maybe it's taking in local street art or sitting in the middle of a busy plaza listening to people speak in a foreign language. You might also appreciate the quiet time alone at night when you can relive your experiences and journal about your accomplishments.

If you haven't travelled by yourself before, try a short break away not too far from home. This could be a weekend visit to somewhere a couple of hours away, or a trip with a friend where you each spend a day or two going your separate ways. Or, how about a retreat, where alone time is built into the agenda? Build up your confidence with shorter trips and work your way towards foreign travel.

Search for solo traveller tips online on sites such as solotravelerworld.com.

To stay connected while travelling alone:

- Join group tours, stay in hostels and chat to locals to maintain some human connection. In fact, you're more likely to get to know others if you're travelling solo, rather than only communicating with your friends, family or group. Find out what locals love about the place you're visiting so you can experience it through their eyes.

- Blog about your adventures or post locations on social media. This can help you feel like you have others with you on your journey even as you make your journey solo.

STAYiNG SAFE

In 1998, Heather Gibson, a sociologist at the University of Florida College of Health and Human Performance, studied the challenges women travellers and solo travellers faced, especially related to safety concerns and objections from family and friends. Today the world is still not completely safe for solo or group travellers, but technology and the expansion of Wi-Fi access has opened up more possibilities for individuals to feel comfortable travelling solo, with the knowledge that they can easily connect to their faraway friends if needed.

There are apps that allow you to create a list of emergency contacts who will be alerted with your GPS coordinates if you press the SOS button or those that give you tips on what to do in the case of more than a dozen different types of emergency, together with a kit of emergency first-aid information.

Some apps have a more global focus, providing alerts about travel alerts in more than 200 countries, plus posts from other travellers who can alert you to potential dangers like pickpockets in the area where you are travelling.

SOLO EATING

Eating has often been viewed as a communal activity; a way to bond with your friends, to express your cultural traditions and celebrate your familial roots. As such, eating alone was regarded as something to avoid, rather than a deliberate choice, as a sign of loneliness or being unable to attract company. In the past, heads would turn if you arrived at a restaurant alone.

That viewpoint is slowly shifting as more solos are venturing out to restaurants around the world, especially in larger cities where people are more likely to live alone.

In the past three years, many online reservation platforms and apps have seen significant rises in booking for one and many people now feel that solo dining is more acceptable than it was five years ago. This trend seems to be on the rise worldwide. In South Korea, more restaurants are catering to honjoks who want to 'honbap', the term for eating alone, or 'honsul', drink alone. They offer privacy partitions and outlets to charge phones. Traditional South Korean fare, like barbecue, is designed for communal meals so restaurants offer other types of cuisine to solo diners.

Some South Korean honjoks are even seeking creative solutions to the challenge of preparing complex traditional meals for one by reaching out to other honjoks to rotate cooking duties.

While nobody can judge your food choices or whether you're eating with the right fork, at first it can feel strange to eat alone. We're more likely to scroll on our phone or watch TV in between hurried bites than eat in silence at a table.

Digital natives who've grown up with technology, with brains attuned to instant gratification, may feel a greater sense of discomfort about being alone with their food with no screens or other stimuli, as opposed to the more subtle appreciation one can feel after a satisfying meal spent in one's own thoughts.

But distractions create a disconnect between our food and our body, making us less aware of when we've had enough to eat. Mindful conscious eating is an antidote to this.

CONSCIOUS EATING

If you've never eaten alone, take small steps towards doing so and when you are ready, you can see how you feel about dining in a restaurant. Start with five minutes of eating without distractions.

- Prepare your meal and set your place at a table. This is an especially important act if you're used to juggling a plate on your lap in front of a television. You can start shifting your mindset simply by sitting at a table. Maybe light a candle or add a decoration that appeals to you, something that honours your effort to dedicate this meal to being with yourself. Put your phone in another room or turn it off.

- Pay attention to how you're eating. Are you eating fast? If so, eat more slowly. How often do you chew? Can you taste your food more when you slow down and focus on eating consciously? Do you find the meal attractive or colourful? What else do you notice?

- Consider how the food affects your body. Does it give you energy, vitality and focus or does it create brain fog, fatigue and bloating? Do you eat when you're hungry or tired? Do your emotions and moods affect how you eat?

HONJOK LIVING

It takes courage to be alone. We risk discovering who we are beyond tribal thinking and our established identity. But it's a powerful act to invest in being alone without distractions. Distractions are a way of hiding from the exploration of our true selves. When we surrender to the art of being alone, we discover how to belong to ourselves through the acceptance of what we discover.

To belong to ourselves means that we can experience the uniqueness of our true selves. We stand alone in our uniqueness. This includes the expression of our gifts.

TUNING INTO OURSELVES

Honjok invites us to upgrade our limited belief systems about who we think we are supposed to be in contrast to who we really are. It's an invitation to uncover what matters most to us, what we truly wish to prioritize in our lives, so that we may incorporate as much alone time as we need or desire.

Invest in exploring what's right for you, whether you live alone or not. Living alone isn't the only way to have an enriched alone experience, you can find true value in being alone even if you live with others.

The real richness comes from being alone with oneself, from that feeling of belonging to yourself that you can only realize through contemplative time.

Understand that the way you choose to spend your alone time may change and shift over time, depending on the stage of your life, the people around you, the limitations you may encounter and your preferences for different activities. Create space for that too.

When we participate in activities with others, it can be more difficult to notice the world around us. We're too busy focusing on and communicating with them. Equally, when we're alone but busy we can find ourselves distracted, either by the task at hand or by ruminating on the past or worrying about the future. What kind of life might we lead if we weren't sleepwalking through our routines and habits or so busy planning ahead that we're not focused on the present?

Alone time can be restful or restorative, energizing or relaxing. Taking part in social activities solo allows you to get to know others or yourself better. The wonderful thing about living a honjok lifestyle is that YOU decide how much time you spend going out or going inwards; where you go and what you do is entirely up to you. It's a way of claiming freedom; a way of stepping away from the 'shoulds' of society and the expectations of others. If you find embarking on this journey difficult, here are some tips to get you started:

- Go for a walk alone without your phone. Pay attention to your surroundings as if you haven't seen them before. Pay attention to your senses – the smells, sights and sounds.

- Try to visit a café once a week by yourself. Put away your phone and try just sitting, watching and thinking. Acknowledge your feelings around being alone in a café. Do you worry about how others are looking at you? How can you let go of other people's judgements?

- Enrol in a class by yourself to explore an activity you've never tried. Even in a group class, you can be pushed out of your comfort zone by not knowing anyone else in the room. You could join a hiking or photography group, or a cooking or pottery class.

- Build from there. Go to a concert, a play or a sporting event on your own. Go on a retreat solo, then book a holiday.

● Spend time cherishing your alone time at home. Look out of your window and observe what you see, hear and feel. Turn on your favourite music and dance around the room. Take pictures of anything that interests you in your area. Curl up in your favourite chair, sip a cup of tea and just be still.

Invest in the preciousness of your own wellbeing. That is what quiet offers. Make solitude a priority, not an indulgence that can wait until you're ready. Find out what activities spark your joy, what allows you to feel free to be yourself and be truly seen for who you are – as an individual.

'And all I loved, I loved alone.'
— EDGAR ALLAN POE

PICTURE CREDITS

Shutterstock, Inc: Pages 2, 4, 19, 25, 30, 44, 45, 48, 50, 57, 58, 66, 68-69, 70, 73, 76, 81, 88, 90, 92, 96, 98-99, 100, 103, 104, 106, 113, 117, 122-123, 124, 127, 129, 130, 132, 136, 138, 140-141, 144, 149, 156 Ji-eun Lee; Page 15 Dawool; Pages 16-17, 35, 47, 62-65, 142 Woocat; 146 Yummyphotos; additional graphics Lucy Palmer

PUBLISHER CREDITS

The publisher would like to thank Seungkwan Chae, Cheryl Rickman and David Eldridge for their help on this project.

Managing Director Lisa Dyer
Senior Commissioning Editor Victoria Marshallsay
Additional text Cheryl Rickman
Copy editors Helen Ridge and Katie Hewett
Proofreader Jane Donovan
Designer Lucy Palmer
Index Angie Hipkin
Production Gary Hayes